Farmer Best Friend

by Myka-Lynne Sokoloff
illustrated by Sophie Hanton

Every day, Farmer White milked Cow and got Hen's eggs. He took out the trash and put Goat in the field to graze.

But one day, he tripped and broke his leg!

"We will help," said Fox with a smile. "I'll get the eggs."

"I'll milk Cow," said Cat.

"We'll take care of the trash," said the mice.

"And I'll just go graze somewhere," said Goat.

"Fine," said Farmer White. "I do need some time to rest."

He sat down and began to play a tune on his fiddle.

The next day, Dog saw that Fox had taken the eggs. Cat had lapped up the milk. Goat had eaten the garden. And the mice had gotten into the trash.

"I'm in charge now," said Dog.

"But you like to sleep and play all day, Dog," said Cat.

"I'm man's best friend," said Dog, "and he needs my help."

Dog got to work. He made sure Cat didn't drink Cow's milk. He made sure Fox didn't steal Hen's eggs. And he made Goat eat the trash instead of the garden.

After a while, Farmer White's leg got better. But he still liked to play the fiddle.

Everyone had a fine old time.